Motherhood is the most wonderful gift nature has bestowed on women. The birth of your little one makes you enter a new phase of life; one that is both rewarding as well as challenging.

The book is divided into three broad sections according to the age of the baby. Upto the age of 4 months, the child is best fed on mother's milk. Tips and recipes for 5-6 months old till the baby turns 2 years are given in this book.

Since it is always advisable to prepare fresh food for the baby, the recipes are very simple and quick to prepare. They have been worded very clearly, so that the food you prepare for your baby is just right in texture and flavour.

All recipes have been created with utmost care to help your child have a nutritionally sound diet.

Enjoy seeing your child grow up well! Nita Mehta

Foreword by Nita Mehta

contents

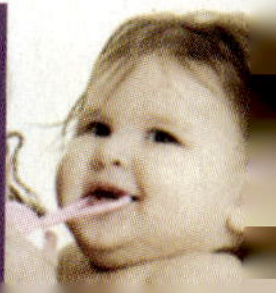

age 5-6 months

Handy Tips for 5-6 Months

- There is no set age at which solid foods must be introduced. This varies from baby to baby depending on the weight gain pattern, baby's digestion, bowel movements etc. Most babies show a readiness for solids between 5-6 months.
- The utensils, preparation surfaces used for cooking for the baby must be absolutely clean. Wash your hands well before you start to prepare any meals for your baby. Make sure that your nails are well trimmed and clean.
- Always keep your baby's utensils separate and rinse it thoroughly with filtered/boiled water before serving any meals.
- While buying feeding utensils for your baby, ensure that you do not buy the cheap, though attractive feeding bowls. Always ensure that the feeding utensils are made of steel or foodgrade materials. It helps if the spoon used for feeding the baby is narrow mouthed and as flat as possible so that it is easy for the baby to scoop out the contents.
- While introducing any new food, start with a teaspoonful and gradually progress to more quantity. Also remember to follow the '4 day rule' when introducing a new food i.e. offer the baby the same food for 4 days to test for allergies and do not introduce more than 1 new food at a time.

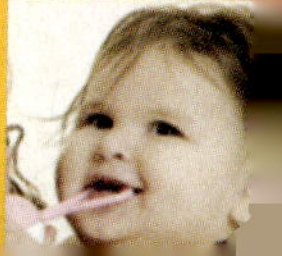

Handy Tips for 5-6 Months

- In some recipes cooked rice has been used. To get ½ cup well cooked, soft rice, wash ¼ cup raw rice. Soak in ¾ cup water for 15 minutes. Put on fire. Bring to a boil. Cover and cook on low heat for 8-10 minutes till rice is done and the water is absorbed.
- It is always advisable to prepare fresh baby food. If, however, food is prepared in advance, it should be cooled quickly and then stored in the fridge.
- Also, if your baby leaves any food in his bowl after a meal, do not preserve it for feeding to the baby later as food that has been in contact with saliva (from your baby's mouth or a feeding spoon) will contain bacteria that will multiply if kept.
- You will often find when you add solid foods to your baby's diet that her stools may change colour and odour. This is normal. If your baby's stools are so firm that they seem to be giving her pain, talk to your doctor for advice, and switch from those types of foods to other fruits and vegetables. You can also offer a little more fluid, such as a few sips of boiled and cooled water to which 1 teaspoon sugar has been added.
- Always remember to check the taste and temperature of the food that you are about to serve your baby.
- If you plan to travel with your baby, always carry food and water for the baby with you. Invest in quality food grade plastic ware to store baby's food.

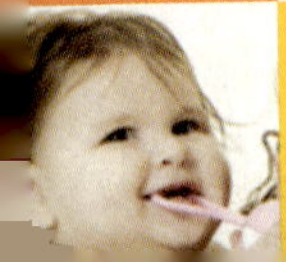

Banana Pudding

You will need...

- 1 ripe banana (the banana should be fully ripe)
- 4 tsp milk
- tiny pinch of cardamom powder (may be added after 6 months)
- 2 glucose biscuits (may be added after 6 months)

How to make it...

1. Peel the ripe banana.
2. Cut into small pieces.
3. Blend into a puree in a blender or mash using a clean strainer.
4. Add warm milk and mix thoroughly.

Tip

For babies older than 6 months, break 2 glucose biscuits and soak in 4 tsp hot milk so that the biscuits crumble completely. Add the banana puree and cardamom powder to make a tasty pudding.

Apple Stew

You will need...

- 1 medium sized apple
- 1 cup water
- ½ tsp sugar (optional)
- tiny pinch of cinnamon for flavouring (after 9 months)

How to make it...

1. Peel, core and cut apple into thin slices.
2. Put the apple pieces in a pan with enough water to cover the apple pieces.
3. Boil (partially covered) till apples are tender.
4. Use a fork to lift the steamed apples and use a clean strainer to puree the apples while mashing the pieces.
5. Use any left over water to thin out the apple puree if so required.
6. The apple stew may be fed as such as first food or also to thicken baby cereal and make it more nutritious.

Tip

In case puree is to be sweetened (depending on the taste of apple used), add sugar. Feed immediately, for it starts to darken on standing.

MICKEY
MICKEY

Makhana Kheer

You will need...

- ½ cup (10-12) puffed lotus seeds (makhanas)
- 1 tsp ghee for roasting
- ½ cup milk
- 1 tsp sugar
- pinch of cardamom powder (optional)

How to make it...

1. Heat 1 tsp ghee in a kadhai. Add makhanas.
2. Roast the makhanas on low flame for 3-4 minutes till the makhanas are crisp.
3. Crush into a powder using a grinder/food processor.
4. Put the ground makhana powder in a pan.
5. Add ½ cup milk and boil the milk on low flame for 6-7 minutes while stirring constantly till the mixture has thickened.
6. Add sugar and cardamom powder (optional). Serve warm.

Tip

If you wish to loosen up the consistency to suit your baby, you may add spoons of hot water before taking the kheer off the flame.

Tip

a. You can add fruit purees (apple or banana or papaya) to make it more tasty and wholesome.
b. To obtain rice powder, grind rice grains in a blender or food processor. Sift through a fine strainer.

Homemade Rice Cereal

You will need...

- ¼ cup rice powder
- 1 cup water
- ½ cup milk (formula or expressed breast milk)
- 1 tsp sugar

How to make it...

1. Bring the water to boil in a sauce pan.
2. Add rice powder while stirring constantly.
3. Simmer for at least 5-7 minutes while whisking constantly. Add 1 tsp sugar.
4. Add the milk slowly and let simmer for 5 minutes on slow flame. Serve warm.

Rice is normally the first cereal to be fed to a baby as it is least likely to trigger any allergic reactions.

c. You can vary this recipe slightly to make rice kanji which is especially invaluable in episodes of upset tummies (diarrohea). For this, boil 1 cup water and add 30 grams (or 2 tbsp) of rice powder to make the solution into a thin liquid. Add one teaspoon of salt and water to this liquid to make it up to 1 litre. Feed as per requirement from time to time.

Clear Moong Dal

You will need...

- 4 tsp split, husked moong beans (dhuli moong dal)
- 1½ cups water
- ¼ tsp of salt, pinch of turmeric (haldi)
- ½ tsp ghee
- few seeds of cumin (jeera)
- small pinch of asafoetida (hing)

How to make it...

1. Wash the moong dal thoroughly.
2. Put in a pressure cooker. Add water, salt & haldi.
3. Put on medium flame. After 1 whistle, reduce flame. After another whistle on low flame, remove from flame.
4. Heat ghee. Add few (5-6) seeds of jeera & a tiny amount of hing. Remove from fire.
5. Add to the dal. Mix thoroughly so that a uniform consistency of dal is obtained. Serve warm.

Moong dal is usually the first of lentils to be introduced in an infant's diet. Once the baby gets used to this, other dals such as arhar or masoor as well as khichri can be introduced.

Tip

a. Before feeding, the jeera seeds can be removed with a spoon.
b. If a thin consistency is required, depending on the baby, the dal can be strained through a strainer.

Moong Dal Khichri

You will need...

for Khichri

- 3 tsp split, husked moong beans (dhuli moong dal)
- 1 tsp rice-soaked for 10 mins
- 2 cups water
- salt
- turmeric to taste
- ½ tomato

for Tadka

- 1 tsp ghee
- a pinch of asafoetida (hing)
- 5-6 seeds of cumin (jeera)

How to make it...

1. Put all the ingredients of the khichri in a pressure cooker after washing the dal and rice thoroughly. Keep the flame high. After 1 whistle reduce the flame and wait for 2 more whistles. Remove from fire. When the pressure drops, remove the skin of tomato and discard skin. Mash the tomato thoroughly.
2. Take 1 tsp ghee in a small tadka kadhai. Add pinch of hing and few jeera seeds.
3. Add the tadka to the khichri and mix thoroughly. Feed warm.

Tip

a. You can add a couple of pieces of apple in the cooker too and mash well before feeding.
b. This light khichri is fed not only in the first year but is also invaluable in episodes of upset tummies for older babies.

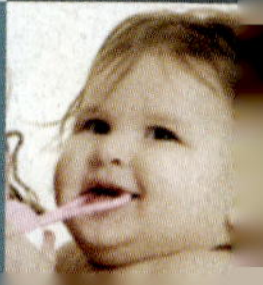

Sooji Upma

You will need...

- 1 tsp ghee
- 1½ tbsp semolina (sooji)
- 1½ cups boiled water
- ¼ tsp salt

How to make it...

1. Heat ghee in a kadhai.
2. Add sooji and bhuno while on medium flame, stirring for 2-3 minutes till sooji begins to change color to light brown.
3. Add salt and hot water and mix while stirring, thoroughly on low flame till the right feeding consistency for your baby is obtained.

Sooji suits the digestion and taste of a young baby very well. This is one of the two basic ways of feeding sooji to a young infant, the other being sooji kheer. Later, these recipes may be enhanced by adding a variety of other ingredients.

Tip

a. After 6 months of age, you can grate half a cheese cube and add before feeding.
b. Sooji preparations become lumpy fast so it is a good idea to prepare immediately before baby's meal time and cool by stirring with a spoon at the time of feeding.

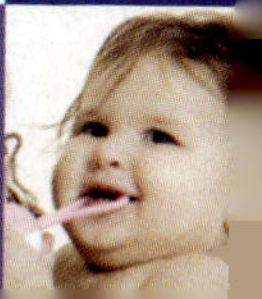

Sooji Kheer

You will need...

- 1 tsp ghee
- 1½ tbsp semolina (sooji)
- 1½ cups hot water, approx.
- 2 tsp sugar
- pinch of green cardamom (chhoti illaichi) powder (optional)
- 1 tsp almond/cashewnut powder (after 6 months)

How to make it...

1. Heat ghee in a kadhai.
2. Add sooji and continue to roast, while continuously stirring, for 5-7 minutes till sooji turns light brown.
3. Add hot water and mix thoroughly.
4. Add sugar and cardamom powder (optional), almond/cashewnut powder.
5. Leave on flame for 5-7 minutes till desired consistency is achieved.
6. Make sure that the sooji kheer is brought down to right temperature before feeding.

Tip

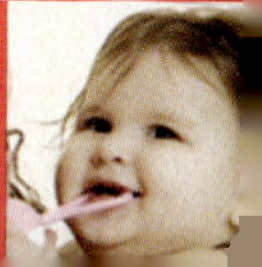

a. You can add milk instead of water (1 cup milk and ½ cup water) or add 1 scoop of milk formula to thicken the kheer.
b. After 1 year sugar can be replaced by honey.
c. After the baby develops taste for this, you can add apple puree/banana puree/papaya puree to it.

Lentils & Vegetable Soup

You will need...

- ½ carrot - peeled & cut into long, thin slices
- ¼ of a potato - cut into 1" pieces
- 2 pieces of lauki, each about 1" big
- 1 tsp split husked moong beans (dhuli moong dal)
- 2 cups water

How to make it...

1. Put the vegetable pieces and dal in a pressure cooker.
2. Add water and put on medium flame.
3. Remove from flame after 1 whistle.
4. After the pressure releases, strain the vegetable pieces and dal and put in a blender.
5. Add a few spoons of water used for cooking so as to obtain the right feeding consistency for your baby. Make the soup slightly thick.
6. Add a pinch of salt and butter and feed.

Tip

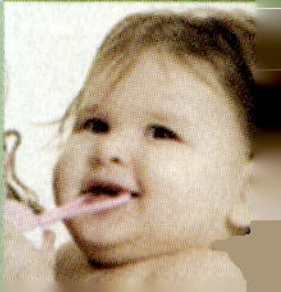

a. You can add grated cheese to the soup for taste variation (Dairy cheese is normally introduced after 6 months of age)
b. The other vegetables that can be used here are sweet potato or peas. Vegetables like cauliflower or cabbage or onion or spinach are strong tasting and are usually introduced after 6-8 months of age

Papaya Puree

You will need...

- 6 chunks of papaya
- 1 cup water
- ½ tsp sugar (optional)

How to make it...

1. Take 6 chunks of a fully ripe papaya.
2. Peel, de-seed and put the pieces in a pan.
3. Add water to cover the papaya chunks.
4. Gently cook, partially covered on a low flame till pieces are very soft. Use a clean strainer to puree the steamed chunks.
5. Add sugar (optional).

Tip

a. Gentle cooking helps break down the sugars and fibres of the fruit for easier digestion by the infant. This need not be required after 7-8 months after which the puree may be obtained by putting ripe papaya pieces in a blender.
b. You can add 2 scoops of milk powder and 60 ml (¼ cup) water to the puree to obtain a yummy papaya smoothie.

age 7–10 months

Handy Tips for 7-10 Months

- Your baby is now probably old enough to sit up on her own and be fed in a highchair or a feeding chair. Ideally, babies this age should be seated with the family at meal times even if they are being served separate food.

- The baby should now be gradually shifted from pureed foods to foods of mashed or slightly lumpy consistency. The baby may occasionally choke a little but a sip of water or a pat behind the neck solves the problem.

- Fruit juices, a variety of lentils, strong tasting vegetables like cabbage, cauliflower, spinach and fruits like mango etc. can now be added.

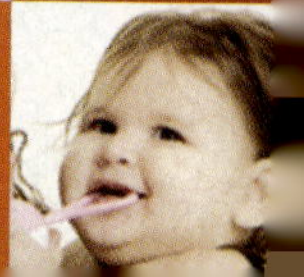

Milky Bread Cubes

You will need...

- 1 slice brown bread
- ½ cup (100 ml) milk
- 1 tbsp custard powder (vanilla or any other flavour)
- 1 tsp sugar
- pinch of cardamom powder

How to make it...

1. Take 2 tbsp of cold milk and mix in the custard powder well to get a thick paste.
2. Put the remaining milk in a heavy bottom pan and bring to boil.
3. Add custard paste to the boiling milk and keep stirring on low flame for 3-4 minutes till the milk begins to thicken.
4. Add sugar & cardamom powder. Remove from fire.
5. Bring to room temperature and spread on a deep saucer.
6. Neatly cut the bread slice into small cubes after cutting off the edges. Immerse each bread piece in the custard prepared above.
   Serve piece by piece.

Soya & Wheat Khichri

You will need...

- 1 cup split, husked moong beans (dhuli moong dal)
- ½ cup yellow lentils (arhar dal)
- 1/3 cup red lentil (masoor dal)
- ¼ cup cracked wheat (dalia)
- 2 tbsp soya granules ground
- 2 cups rice

Mix the above and store in an airtight container. Use for preparing khichri as mentioned.

How to make it...

1. Take about 4 tbsp of the mix and after thorough washing, put in pressure cooker.
2. Add sufficient water (2½ cups), pinch of salt, turmeric. Add one half of a small tomato (without slicing) and put the pressure cooker on fire. After 1 whistle on high flame, reduce the flame to minimum and wait for 2-3 more whistles. Remove from pressure and let the pressure drop.
3. For 'tadka', take ½ tsp ghee, few jeera seeds, pinch of hing & add to the khichri on release of pressure.
4. Lift the tomato so as to neatly extract out its skin. Discard skin and mash the remaining pulp into the khichri.
5. Mash the khichri with a heavy spoon to achieve the desired consistency.

Tip

a. You may add 1 dollop of fresh curd for taste variation.
b. Add 3-4 drops of lemon juice to occasionally alter the taste.
c. Add cubes of lauki or apple or potato to the mix at the time of putting in the pressure cooker and mash thoroughly after cooking.

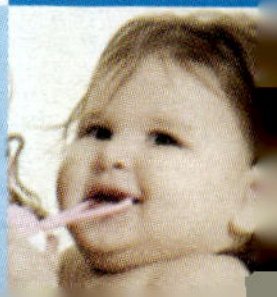

Tip

a. Mangoes are usually introduced in the second half of the baby's first year. They need not be steamed as at this age, most babies can tolerate raw foods. However, if the baby's digestion is somewhat frail, mangoes too can be steamed and pureed

Mango Masti

You will need...

- 1 ripe mango
- ½ cup well cooked rice
- ½ cup plain curd - beat well till smooth

How to make it...

1. Peel, de-seed and mash the mango using a blender.
2. Strain the mango puree to remove fibre threads.
3. Add ½ cup fresh curd and mix thoroughly.
4. Add the cooked rice and mix while slightly mashing in with a fork.

b. Tiny dices of ripe mango make for a great finger food and can be fed as such to babies older than 9 months.

Curd Rice

You will need...

- ½ cup well cooked rice
- 1 cup fresh curd
- 1 tsp sugar or puree of mango or banana or rooh afza

How to make it...

1. Take ½ cup well cooked warm rice in a bowl.
2. Add 1 cup fresh curd. Mash lightly with a fork.
3. Add sugar or fruit puree or 1 tsp of rooh afza.

This simple preparation usually suits the palate of most babies and is very filling and easy to digest too.

Tip

Alternatively, the baby can be fed the popular south Indian version of curd rice modified to suit babies. For this, wash, soak and boil the rice. Keep it aside. Beat the curd and add salt to taste. Gently mix it with the cooked rice. For the seasoning, take a little hot ghee and splutter few mustard seeds (sarson) in it. Pour over rice mix. Mix well. Serve cold.

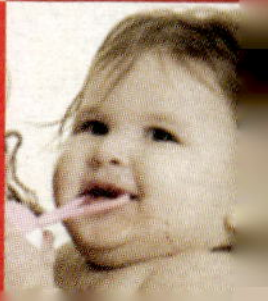

ICE CREAM

Nutritious Porridge

You will need...

- 3 tsp cracked wheat (dalia)
- 1 tsp ghee
- ½ medium tomato - grated
- ½ medium onion - grated
- 2" piece of lauki - grated (¼ cup)
- ¼ tsp almond/cashewnut powder
- ½ cheese cube - grated
- ¼ tsp salt

How to make it...

1. Heat ½ tsp ghee in a kadhai. Add dalia. Bhuno the dalia for 2 minutes. Remove from flame. Keep the dalia separately.
2. Again heat ½ tsp ghee in the kadhai and add the finely grated onion. Keep stirring till the onion start to turn golden.
3. Add the finely grated lauki and tomato. Stir the mix for 2-3 minutes and add salt.
4. Add the roasted dalia and 1 cup water, cover partially and leave on low flame for approximately 10 minutes till the dalia is well cooked.
5. Add almond/cashewnut powder as well as grated cheese.
6. Adjust consistency by adding water if thinner consistency is required. Serve with a dollop of fresh curd.

Fruity Combos (Rich in Iron)

You will need...

- 1 ripe cheeku (should be soft to touch)
- ½ banana
- 1 cup milk

How to make it...

1. Mix together the ingredients in a blender.
2. Strain to remove any lumpy pieces. Serve.

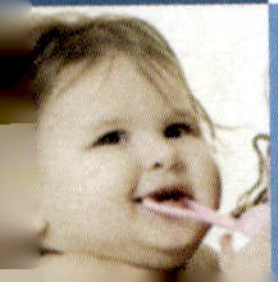

Egg (Soft Boil)

You will need...

- 1 egg
- 2 cups water for boiling

How to make it...

1. Put 2 cups water in a sauce pan. Gently place the egg and let boil on a high flame. As soon as the water starts boiling, reduce flame.
2. For getting a soft boiled egg, switch off flame after 2 minutes. Deshell carefully. Take only the yellow portion of the egg. Add a tiny pinch of salt and feed.
3. If you wish to loosen up the consistency, add a couple of teaspoons of hot water or milk and feed.

Tip

a. A baby is usually fed only the egg yellow in the first year, egg whites which are more likely to trigger allergies are normally introduced in the second year.

b. While introducing egg, a baby should ideally be desensitized. For this, on the first day, feed only one spoon of the egg, on the second day feed two teaspoons and so on till after 5 days the baby acquires tolerance to eggs.

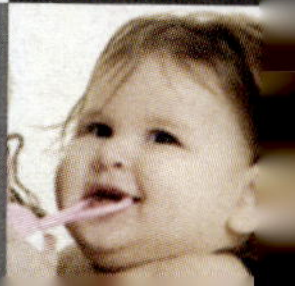

Banana Oats Porridge

You will need...

- 2 tbsp porridge oats
- ¼ cup milk
- ½ banana (ripe) - cut into tiny pieces

How to make it...

1. Place the oats and milk in a milk pan.
2. Bring upto boiling point while stirring occasionally.
3. Lower the heat now and simmer gently uncovered for about 3 minutes till the porridge turns thick and creamy. Remove from fire.
4. Add the banana pieces.
5. Puree the mixture in a blender.
6. Add hot milk to adjust consistency as per the feeding requirement of the baby.

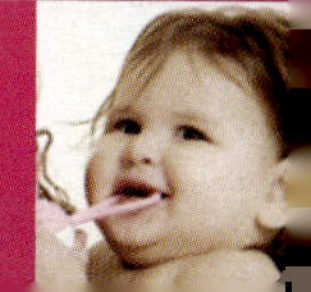

Tasty Potato Mash

You will need...

- 1 medium potato
- 2 tbsp milk
- salt (optional)

How to make it...

1. Peel the potatoes, cut into small pieces and put them to cook with abundant cold water. Alternatively, put in a pressure cooker and wait for 1 whistle on low flame.
2. Once the potato is cooked, mash it thoroughly.
3. Strain while adding in the milk and some liquid from the left over cooking water till the consistency right for your baby is achieved.
4. As the baby gets used to the taste, you can go making it a bit thicker.

Tip

Add 1 tsp of cheese spread or butter to make it more yummy.

Tasty Spinach Soup

You will need...

- 5-6 leaves spinach
- half a tomato (ripe, medium size)
- 1 tbsp curd
- 1½ tbsp cornflour dissolved in ½ cup water
- 1 tsp butter
- salt to taste

How to make it...

1. Thoroughly wash the spinach leaves.
2. Put the leaves along with half a tomato in a cooker. Add 1 cup water and allow 1 whistle. Remove from fire.
3. When the pressure releases remove the vegetables. Remove skin of tomato. Blend peeled tomato and spinach leaves with the water in a mixer to obtain a thick puree.
4. In a pan heat 1 tsp butter. Add the puree.
5. Add the curd and cornflour mix and stir well on low flame for approx 2 minutes. Remove from fire.
6. Add a pinch of salt and a few drops of lemon juice (optional).

Sweet Potatoes with Yogurt

You will need...

- ½ small sweet potato/apple
- 1 tbsp yogurt

How to make it...

1. Boil sweet potato with the peel in water for about 10 minutes or till soft. Peel and mash. If using apple, do not boil. Simply peel and chop finely.
2. Put ½ cup warm sweet potato in a blender or food processor. Add 1 tbsp yogurt. Blend to a puree, adding some boiled water/ formula or breast milk if needed to get a thick and lumpy mixture.

Tip

For older babies, stir in diced fruit, such as apples, peaches or banana.

Semolina & Carrot Porridge

You will need...

- 2 tbsp semolina (sooji/rawa)
- ½ of a small carrot - grated very finely
- ½ cup milk

How to make it...

1. Dry roast semolina in a pan on low heat for 2-3 minutes.
2. Add carrot and milk, cook stirring till it starts to boil. Cook for another minute or till the carrot is soft.
3. Remove from heat. Serve at room temperature.

Rice Phirni

You will need...

- 2 cups milk
- ¼ cup basmati rice
- 3 tbsp mashed fruit (strawberry or apricot or mango)

How to make it...

1. Soak rice in 1 cup water for 3-4 hour. Drain. Grind with 4 to 5 tablespoonfuls of water to a paste. Dissolve the rice paste in ¼ cup milk and make it thin.
2. Mix the rice paste and 1¾ cups milk in a heavy bottomed kadhai. Cook on low heat, for about 5 minutes, stirring continuously, till the mixture is of a thick consistency. Remove from fire.
3. Cool and add the fruit. Serve at room temperature.

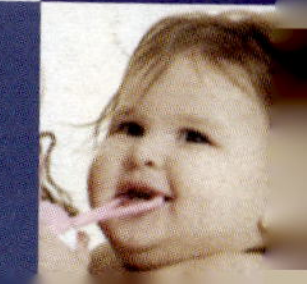

age 11 months - 2 years

Tips for 11 Months - 2 Years

- At this age baby should be taking a variety of cereals, pulses, vegetables and having solid meals 3 times a day.
- The baby will probably try self feeding, at least her favourite dishes, but never leave your baby alone when eating because of the risk of choking.
- Don't give honey until age one because it can carry a small risk of infant botulism.
- Depending upon your infant's diet, vitamin drops may be recommended. Ask your doctor for more advice.
- This is the age when feeding problems may start. To avoid this, do not push too hard while feeding and try and make the mealtime pleasant and an opportunity to bond with your baby.
- At this age the baby's diet needs to be gradually modified so that it eventually merges with the meals prepared for the rest of the family. Thus, Dal-Chawal, Dal-Roti (pieces of soft phulkas soaked in hot dal), Dudh-Roti (pieces of soft phulkas soaked in sweet milk) should be included in the baby's/ toddler's diet. A number of other nutritious recipes for babies/toddlers of this age which can also be enjoyed by older siblings/other family members are given.

Oatmeal and Bananas

You will need...

- ¼ cup instant oats
- ¾ cup water
- 2-3 tbsp chopped banana

How to make it...

1. Combine the oats and water.
2. Bring to a boil, reduce heat and simmer for about 5 minutes. Remove from heat and stir in the banana.

Whole Wheat Chillas

You will need...

- 1 cup whole wheat atta - sifted
- 2 tbsp curd
- 1½ cups water
- ¼ onion - finely chopped (2 tbsp)
- ¾ tsp salt or to taste
- pinch of roasted cumin (bhuna jeera) powder or chaat masala

How to make it...

1. Mix the ingredients thoroughly to make a smooth batter of thickish pouring consistency making sure that all lumps are broken down.
2. Heat 1 tsp oil on a non-stick tawa. Pour 2 tbsp batter and spread into a circle using a spatula keeping the flame low.
3. After about 3-4 minutes, when the sides begin to rise and light brown patches appear on the lower surface turn and cook the other side. Serve with dahi.

For Meetha Chillas

Mix 1 cup whole wheat flour with ½ cup milk. Add enough water to get thick pouring consistency. Add 2 tbsp sugar and 1 tbsp almond powder. Proceed from step 2.

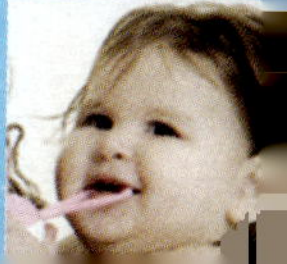

Egg Poach (Fried Egg)

You will need...

- 1 egg
- 1 tbsp oil and salt to taste

How to make it...

1. Use a small thick bottomed pan and put 1 tbsp of oil in it, spread the oil around the pan well.
2. When the pan is hot, break the egg into it and cover the pan. Allow it to cook for 2 to 3 minutes and it is ready to eat.
3. Sprinkle a pinch of salt. Serve.

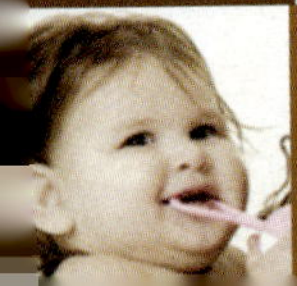

Cottage Cheese Balls

You will need...

- ½ litre full cream milk or 1/3 cup grated ready-made paneer
- lemon for curdling the milk
- 2 tbsp gram flour (besan) - dry roast on a tawa for 2 minutes on low heat
- 2 tbsp whole wheat flour (atta)
- 1 tsp chaat masala
- tiny pinch of pepper

How to make it...

1. Put the milk to boil. As soon as the milk starts to boil, add lemon juice by squeezing lemon through a strainer to discard any seeds.
2. When the milk has completely curdled (1-2 minutes), remove from flame and strain the curdled milk through a muslin cloth. The soft paneer (1/3 cup) will be collected while the liquid can be used to make dal or dough.
3. Add the remaining ingredients to the paneer, mix thoroughly with the palm to make a smooth mixture. Make into small balls.
4. Deep fry 1-2 balls at a time till the balls turn golden brown.

Whole Moong Chillas

You will need...

- 1 cup green moong beans (green saboot moong dal)
- ½ cup chopped green coriander
- 2 tbsp gram flour (besan)
- 2 tbsp curd
- ½ tsp salt to taste
- 1 tsp chaat masala
- ½ onion - chopped very finely

How to make it...

1. Soak moong dal for 8 hours. Drain and grind to paste with coriander, using about ¼ cup water.
2. Add remaining ingredients and mix thoroughly till there are no lumps.
3. Add enough water, about 2 cups, till the batter is of thick pouring consistency.
4. Spread little oil on a nonstick tawa. Take 2 tbsp of batter and spread thinly.
5. Leave on low flame for 3-4 minutes till the sides begin to rise slightly.
6. Turn, cook on the other side. Fold and serve with a dollop of butter or fresh curd.

Tip

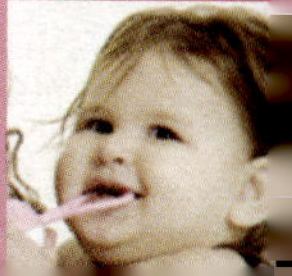

Moong Pakoda

Reduce quantity of water to about ½ cup to get a thick dropping batter. Beat batter well to make it fluffy. Add all ingredients. Drop spoonful in hot oil and deep fry to make pakoras

Whole Wheat Pua

You will need...

- 1 cup whole wheat atta
- ½ ripe banana - chopped finely
- 4 tbsp sugar
- 1 cup milk
- 1 tsp desiccated coconut (fine coconut powder), optional
- 1 tsp fine almond/cashewnut powder

How to make it...

1. Mix the above ingredients in a mixer to prepare a smooth batter.
2. Heat about 5-6 tbsp ghee in a kadhai.
3. Pour 1 tbsp of batter into the ghee and deep fry on slow flame, turning the pua till both sides turn golden brown.
4. Puas made can be easily stored refrigerated for 3-4 days in an air tight container.

Tip

Spread a little bit of fresh malai (milk cream) on the pua to make it more yummy.

Cheese Omelette

You will need...

- 1 egg
- 1 cheese cube (30 gm) - grated
- 1 tsp oil and salt to taste

How to make it...

1. Beat the egg with a fork. Add a big pinch of salt.
2. Heat a small thick bottomed pan. Put oil in it, spread the oil around the pan well. When it is hot, add in the egg mixture.
3. Top up with the grated cheese.
4. When it is almost completely cooked, turn the stove off and cover the omelette for a couple of minutes until it has cooked completely.

Stuffed Paratha

You will need...

for the Dough

- ½ cup whole wheat flour, plus a little extra for dusting
- ½ tsp salt
- 1 tsp oil
- lukewarm water for kneading the dough

for the Stuffing

- one large potato - boiled and mashed
- ½ tsp salt
- ½ tsp chaat masala
- ½ tsp coriander (dhania) powder

Stuffed Paratha (contd.)

How to make it...

For the Dough: Sieve the flour into a mixing bowl and add the salt. Mix oil into the flour. Slowly add lukewarm water and start to mix the dough. The resultant dough should be a firm dough (not as soft as that used for chapatis). Knead it well; cover and leave it for 20 minutes.

For the Parantha:

1. Divide the dough into 2-3 equal sized balls.
2. Roll out each ball into a circular shape about 4 cm in diameter.
3. Place 1 heaped tbsp of the filling mix in the centre of one circle. Fold the edges to enclose the filling, & on a well-floured surface, roll each ball into a bigger, round shape.
4. Heat a non-stick frying pan. Put the parantha onto the heated pan and cook for 1 minute on medium heat until small bubbles appear on the surface. Turn over and cook the other side for 1 minute.
5. Rub the surface with a little oil or ghee and turn it over. Using a heavy spatula, press down evenly over the parantha. Fry it like this for 1 minute. Repeat the same for the other side until the parantha is golden and crisp. Serve warm.

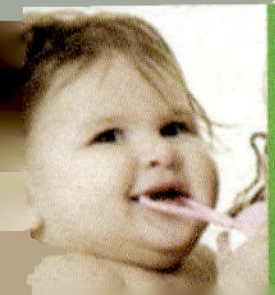

Stuffed Paratha (contd.)

Tip

Numerous other stuffings can be served to babies of this age such as:

1. **Sweet parantha stuffing:** The gourd family of vegetables - pumpkin or bottle gourd, is good for making sweet paranthas. Knead grated pumpkin in the flour. Add grated jaggery or sugar and make the dough with milk, instead of water. Flavour it slightly with a hint of cinnamon (dalchini) powder or cardamom (illaichi).
2. **Carrot Paranthas:** Grate a carrot and lightly fry for 2-3 minutes. Add a pinch of salt and bhuna jeera and mix in the dough while kneading the dough.
3. **Paneer Paranthas:** Use fresh homemade paneer. Add fine chopped coriander leaves, fine grated onion, chaat masala and a few drops of lemon juice. Mix thoroughly. Use as stuffing for paranthas.
4. **Paalak Paranthas:** Take a bunch of spinach leaves and boil. Blend in a mixer along with a cheese cube and a pinch of salt. Use the puree to knead dough instead of adding water. Make paranthas using this dough.
5. **Sattu Paranthas:** Take 1 tbsp sattu, add salt, chaat masala and 1 tsp oil. Mix well and use as stuffing.

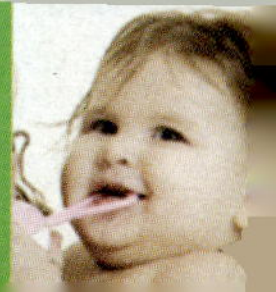

Fresh Chikoo Ice Cream

You will need...

- 200-250 gm fresh ripe chikoo
- 250 gm fresh cream
- 6 tbsp powdered sugar
- 1 tsp gelatine
- ½ tsp vanilla essence
- 2 tbsp raisins, preferably black raisins

How to make it...

1. Peel the chikoo and chop. Grind to a puree. Transfer to a bowl.
2. Soak gelatine in 1 tbsp water in a very small pan for 5 minutes. Stir on very low heat for a few seconds, till it dissolves.
3. Add gelatine to chikoo puree and mix well.
4. Whip cream with powdered sugar till thick.
5. Add chikoo puree to whipped cream. Mix well. Add essence and raisins. Mix and check sugar.
6. Transfer to an ice cream box. Cover with a plastic sheet (cling wrap) and then with the lid. Freeze overnight or till firm.

SUBZIS FOR TODDLERS

Apart from soups and other dishes involving vegetables, when a baby reaches a year he should be introduced to subzis or vegetables cooked the traditional Indian way which serve as an accompaniment with rotis or paranthas. In the beginning it helps if the subzis are gravy based so that the baby can be fed the subzi along with roti or parantha. Here are some subzis which babies this age can be fed and are yummy too. What's more, these are healthy and tasty enough to appeal to older siblings/other family members too!

SUBZIS FOR TODDLERS

Soya Curry

You will need...

- 1 medium sized tomato - grated to remove the skin
- 1 onion - grated
- 1 small potato - boiled and cut into ½" pieces
- 1 tbsp soya granules - soaked in warm water for 10 minutes
- 1½ cups water
- ½ tsp of coriander powder (dhania)
- ½ tsp garam masala (optional)
- a pinch of turmeric (haldi)
- ½ tsp salt, or to taste
- 1 tbsp oil

How to make it...

1. Heat the oil in a kadhai. Add grated onion and bhuno for 2-3 minutes till it turns golden.
2. Add ½ tsp dhania powder and a pinch of haldi. Mix well.
3. Add the grated tomato and mix well.
4. Add the soya granules and boiled potato cut into small cubes.
5. Bhuno for 1 minute and add salt and garam masala (optional). Bhuno again for 2 minutes.
6. Add water. Bring to a boil. Cook covered on medium flame for 3 minutes.
7. Uncover, stir for half a minute and remove from flame.
8. Serve with roti or puri.

NUBY

Potato and Pea Curry

You will need...

- 1 potato - cut into 1" cubes
- ½ cup shelled peas
- 2 tbsp oil
- ¼ tsp turmeric (haldi)
- ¼ tsp garam masala
- ½ tsp ground coriander (dhania powder)
- ½ tsp salt to taste

Grind together

- 2 tomatoes - chopped
- 1 onion - chopped
- 2 flakes garlic
- ½ tsp chopped ginger

How to make it...

1. Heat oil. Add the onion-tomato paste. Cook till dry and oil separates.
2. Add masalas - haldi, garam masala, coriander and salt. Stir for 1 minute.
3. Add potato cubes and stir for 3-4 minutes. Add 1 cup water and bring to a boil.
4. Add peas and simmer covered for 7-8 minutes till potatoes are cooked. Mash the potatoes slightly.
5. Serve with roti or rice.

Palak Paneer

You will need...

- 1 bundle (approx. 400 gm) paalak
- 100 gm fresh paneer (preferably homemade)
- 2 medium sized onions - grated
- 2 medium sized tomatoes - grated
- 1 tsp dhania powder
- pinch of haldi
- salt to taste
- 1 tbsp oil
- ½ tsp ginger-garlic paste

How to make it...

1. Clean thoroughly paalak leaves and boil with ½ cup water for 5 minutes till tender. Puree in a blender.
2. Heat the oil in a kadhai. Add ginger-garlic paste and bhuno for 1 minute.
3. Add grated onion and bhuno for 5-6 minutes till it turns golden.
4. Add 1 tsp dhania powder, salt and a pinch of haldi.
5. Add the grated tomato and mix well. Cook for 2 minutes.
6. Add paalak puree and cook on low flame for 4-5 minutes.
7. Mash the paneer till it crumbles and add to the gravy. Add a dollop of butter and serve with roti.

Any remaining subzi can be used for kneading the dough to make paalak paranthas.

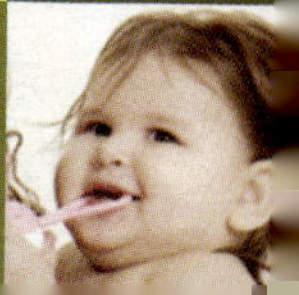

FINGER FOODS

When the baby reaches the age 7-9 months and has a pretty good pincher grasp, he wants to and can pick foods in his hands and suck or munch on them. This should be encouraged as it is a stepping stone to self feeding. At this age it is important that the baby be offered a variety of finger foods which can be as simple as a biscuit, a toast, soup stick, boiled carrot cubes or cooked pasta or even a cheese slice. When you wish you can try out something more filling. These recipes will make a good choice. One thing to remember when your baby is eating finger foods or eating with his hands, remember to wash his hands well before he eats his meals.

Vegetable Fry

You will need...

- 5-6 small florets of cauliflower or 3-4 lady's finger or quarter of capsicum (medium size) - cut into thin small strips
- oil for deep frying
- salt/chaat masala to taste

How to make it...

1. Heat 2 tbsp oil in a kadhai. When the oil is heated, add the vegetables.
2. Keep on stirring briskly for approximately 4 minutes on medium heat till the vegetables are done and crisp.
3. Take out the veg fries and spread on a plate.
4. Add a sprinkle of salt/chaat masala and offer warm.

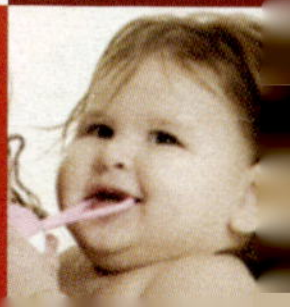

Raw Banana Chips

You will need...

- 1 medium sized raw banana
- salt to taste
- 2 tbsp oil for stir frying

How to make it...

1. Lengthwise cut out the skin of the banana from all sides using a sharp knife.
2. Now slice the banana into thin round pieces.
3. Heat 2 tbsp oil in a non-stick pan and add the slices.
4. Cover and cook for 2 minutes.
5. Remove cover and stir fry for about 2 minutes more, till the slices are cooked crisp. Remove from fire.
6. Remove chips from kadhai. Spread on a plate. Sprinkle a few drops of lemon juice and a pinch of salt. A hint of black pepper powder adds to the taste. Serve immediately.

Soft Idlis

You will need...

- 1 cup split black gram (dhuli urad dal)
- 1 cup sela (parboiled) rice
- 1 cup permal rice
- ½ tsp fenugreek seeds (methi dana)
- oil for greasing mould
- salt to taste

How to make it...

1. Soak the urad dal and methi seeds in water for at least 4 hours. Separately soak both rice in water for at least 4 hours.
2. Grind the dal to a fine paste. Next grind the rice together into a coarse paste. Now mix both the pastes well and add salt. Cover and keep overnight.
3. Next morning, mix the batter well. Grease the idli moulds before pouring the batter. Fill the moulds about ¾ and then steam them for about 15 minutes. After awhile, open the idli cooker and demould the hot, steaming idlis with the help of a blunt knife. Cut into small pieces and serve to the baby.

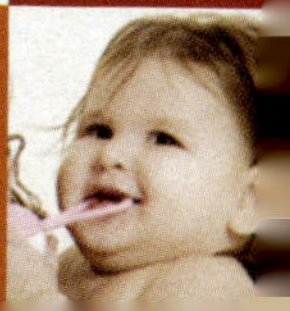

Besan ki Burfi

You will need...

- 250 gm (2¾ cups) gram flour (besan)
- 150 gm (1¼ cup) powdered sugar
- 150 gm (¾ cup) pure ghee
- seeds of 3-4 green cardamoms (chhoti illaichi) - powdered

How to make it...

1. In a heavy bottomed kadhai, put besan. Dry roast besan for about 10 minutes on low heat, stirring continuously till fragrant & gives out a roasted smell.
2. Add ghee. Cook on very low heat for about 15 minutes till the besan turns golden. Do not make it brown. Make it just golden with a hint of brown.
3. Remove from fire. Add sugar and mix well.
4. Transfer to a greased thali. Press well to make the top smooth.
5. Sprinkle illaichi powder. Leave to set for 5-6 hours at room temperature in a cool place but not in the refrigerator. You can leave it over night to set well.
6. Cut into 1" squares and store in an air tight box after it turns absolutely cold.

Soya Bread Rolls

You will need...

- 3 slices brown bread with the edges cut out
- ½ cup milk
- 1 small potato - boiled and mashed
- ½ tsp coriander powder (dhania)
- ½ tsp chaat masala
- ¼ tsp salt, or to taste
- 1 tbsp soya granules

How to make it...

1. Mix all ingredients except bread and milk.
2. Place the milk in a saucer. Wet a slice of bread by dipping in milk for a second. Placing the soaked bread on the palm of one hand, press bread with other palm to pat out excess milk.
3. Place a tbsp of mixture in the centre in oblong shape. Fold over remaining slice and press well to seal. Roll between palms gently taking care that there are no openings where filling will pop out so that a smooth roll is obtained.
4. Heat oil nicely and slide in prepared roll, deep fry on medium heat till it turns golden. Cut into smaller pieces and serve with sauce or chutney.

French Toast Cubes

You will need...

- 1 egg, salt to taste
- 1 slice brown bread
- 1 tbsp milk
- oil to fry

How to make it...

1. Break the egg into a cup. Beat well, add salt and pour onto a plate.
2. Cut out the edges of the bread and cut into 4 squares.
3. Pour the milk onto a plate and dip the bread pieces in it briefly. Gently squeeze out the extra milk and keep aside.
4. Now dip the bread pieces into the egg mixture.
5. Heat oil in a frying pan and deep fry the pieces till it starts to turn light brown.
6. Serve with sauce.

A delicious sweet version of this can be obtained by beating the egg along with the milk, 1 teaspoon sugar, a pinch of ground cinnamon powder. You can take 1 tbsp cornflakes and crumble it and add to the egg mix to make a crunchy sweet French toast.

Soya Pakoras

You will need...

- 10-12 soya chunks
- 2 tbsp gram flour (besan)
- 2 tbsp atta
- oil for deep frying
- ¼ tsp salt

How to make it...

1. Boil 2 cups water in a pan. Add soya chunks. Remove from fire. Cover the vessel with a lid. Leave it aside for 10 minutes. Rinse with cold water, drain water from the chunks and squeeze lightly.
2. Mix besan and atta with ¼ tsp salt. With about ¼ cup water, make a paste. Dip soya chunks to coat thoroughly.
3. Heat oil in a kadhai. Deep fry these soya chunks and serve.

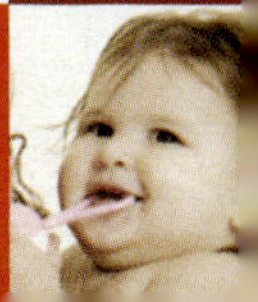

Atta Besan Laddu

You will need...

- 2 cups whole wheat flour (atta)
- 1 cup gram flour (besan)
- 1 cup powdered sugar, preferably bura sugar
- ¼ cup finely chopped mixed dry fruits (almonds, raisins, kaju etc.)
- ¾ cup ghee

How to make it...

1. Heat ghee in a kadhai. Add atta and besan. Roast on very low heat for about 15 minutes, stirring constantly, till the flour changes colour and gives out a fragrant roasted smell. Remove from fire.
2. Add finely chopped dry fruits in the mixture.
3. Add ground sugar and mix thoroughly. Make balls. Let them cool to room temperature. Store in an air tight box.

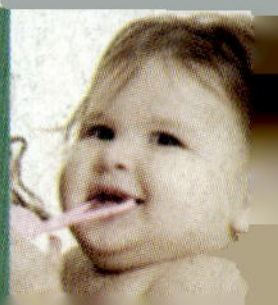

Sabodana Faces

You will need...

- 4 potatoes-boiled & mashed
- ½ cup sago (sabodana) - soak in 1 cup warm water for 1 hour
- 2 tsp poppy seeds (khus-khus)
- ½ cup cornflour
- ½ tsp chaat masala
- 1 medium onion - chopped finely
- 2 tbsp chopped green coriander
- ½ tsp garam masala
- ½ tsp red chilli powder
- ½ tsp amchoor
- salt to taste

How to make it...

1. Soak sabodana in about 1 cup warm water to cover it for ½-1 hour or till soft. Drain and wash in running water to keep them separate. Strain.
2. Mix mashed potatoes and all the other ingredients, except pepper corns and ketchup. Mix well to get a tikki mixture.
3. Shape into 12 balls. Flatten each ball and press 2 peppercorns like two eyes.
4. Deep fry 2-3 pieces in a kadhai at a time in medium hot oil till golden. Make a mouth shape with ketchup. Serve hot.

Decoration: 10-12 whole pepper corns (saboot kali mirch), some tomato ketchup in a squeeze bottle

Crunchy Pattise

You will need...

- 1 cup cracked wheat (dalia)
- 1 cup boiled and mashed potatoes (2 potatoes)
- 1 tsp salt
- ¼ tsp red chilli powder
- 1 tsp coriander (dhania) powder
- ½ tsp garam masala
- 1 tsp dry mango (amchoor) powder
- 2-3 tbsp chopped coriander leaves

To serve: hung yogurt mixed with some hari chutney or ketchup

How to make it...

1. Soak dalia in water for 1 hour. Strain. Squeeze out excess water by pressing well in the strainer with a kadchi. Transfer to a bowl.
2. Mix mashed potatoes and all other ingredients to the dalia. Mix well.
3. Form into 1½" patties shape. Flatten sides and shallow fry 1 or 2 pieces at a time in hot oil till golden brown.
4. Serve hot dotted with hung yogurt mixed with some hari chutney.

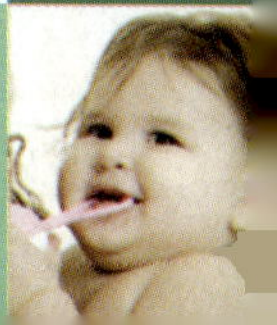

Glossary of Names/Terms

Hindi or English names as used in India	Used in USA/UK/other countries
Baingan	Eggplant, aubergine
Bhutta	Corn
Capsicum	Bell peppers
Chhoti Illaichi	Green cardamom
Chilli powder	Red chilli powder, Cayenne pepper
Cornflour	Cornstarch
Dalchini	Cinnamon
French beans	Green beans
Gobhi	Cauliflower
Hara Dhania	Cilantro/fresh or green coriander leaves
Hari Gobhi	Broccoli
Hari Mirch	Green hot peppers, green chillies
Imli	Tamarind
Jeera	Cumin seeds
Saunf	Fennel
Sela Chaawal	Parboiled rice, which when cooked is not sticky at all
Seviyaan	Vermicelli
Soda-bi-carb	Baking soda
Til	Sesame seeds
Toned Milk	Milk with 1% fat content
Yellow Capsicum	Yellow bell peppers

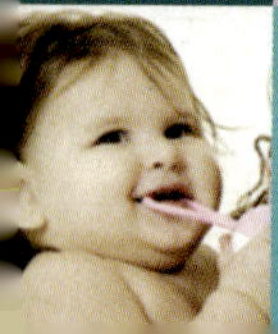

International Conversion Guide

Weights & Measures

Metric	Imperial
15 g	½ oz
30 g	1 oz
60 g	2 oz
90 g	3 oz
125 g	4 oz (¼ lb)
155 g	5 oz
185 g	6 oz
220 g	7 oz
250 g	8 oz (½ lb)
280 g	9 oz
315 g	10 oz
345 g	11 oz
375 g	12 oz (¾ lb)
410 g	13 oz
440 g	14 oz
470 g	15 oz
500 g	16 oz (1 lb)
750 g	24 oz (1½ lb)
1 kg	30 oz (2 lb)

Liquid Measures

Metric	Imperial
30 ml	1 fluid oz
60 ml	2 fluid oz
100 ml	3 fluid oz
125 ml	4 fluid oz
150 ml	5 fluid oz (¼ pint/1 gill)
190 ml	6 fluid oz
250 ml	8 fluid oz
300 ml	10 fluid oz (½ pint)
500 ml	16 fluid oz
600 ml	20 fluid oz (1 pint)
1000 ml	1¾ pints

Cups & Spoon Measures

Metric	Imperial
1 ml	¼ tsp
2 ml	½ tsp
5 ml	1 tsp
15 ml	1 tbsp
60 ml	¼ cup
125 ml	½ cup
250 ml	1 cup

Helpful Measures

Metric	Imperial
3 mm	1/8 in
6 mm	¼ in
1 cm	½ in
2 cm	¾ in
2.5 cm	1 in
5 cm	2 in
6 cm	2½ in
8 cm	3 in
10 cm	4 in
13 cm	5 in
15 cm	6 in
18 cm	7 in
20 cm	8 in
23 cm	9 in
25 cm	10 in
28 cm	11 in
30 cm	12 in (1ft)

Breakfast Recipes Veg.

Paneer Recipes Veg.

Paranthas & Rice for Kids

Punjabi Recipes Veg.

Pizza & Pasta Veg.

Cooking for Growing Kids

Cooking Under 10 Minutes

Cake Cookbook

Tiffin Recipes for Children

Indian Favourites Veg. Recipe

Chatpati Chaat

Snacks & Chaat

Cakes Cookies

Vegetarian Recipes

Zero Oil Recipes

BEST SELLERS BY SNAB Excellence in Books

baby cookbook

Ideal Cookbook for a New Mother

Author:

Garima Bhagat

Joint Commissioner of Income Tax

Nita Mehta

Cook with Confidence

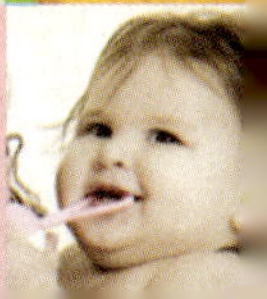

baby cookbook

Ideal Cookbook for a New Mother

Reprint 2010

ISBN 978-81-7676-101-7

Food Styling and Photography: Nita Mehta Cook with Confidence

Layout and Laser Typesetting :

N.I.T.A. ☎ 23252948
National Information Technology Academy
3A/3, Asaf Ali Road
New Delhi-110002

Published by :

Nita Mehta
Cook with Confidence

3A/3 Asaf Ali Road, New Delhi-110002
Tel: 91-11-23250091, 29214011, 23252948

E-Mail: nitamehta@nitamehta.com
Website: http://www.nitamehta.com

Distributed by :

NITA MEHTA BOOKS
3A/3, Asaf Ali Road, New Delhi - 02
Distribution Centre:
D16/1, Okhla Industrial Area, Phase-I,
New Delhi-110020
Tel.: 26813199, 26813200

Printed in India

Contributing Writers :

Anurag Mehta
Tanya Mehta
Subhash Mehta

Editors :
Sangeeta
Sunita

Recipe Development & Testing:

Nita Mehta Foods - R & D Centre
3A/3, Asaf Ali Road, New Delhi-110002
E-143, Amar Colony, Lajpat Nagar-IV
New Delhi-110024

Rs. 89/-